A Mother's Heart

A Mother's Heart

Poetry and Prose to Comfort
a Mother's Heart after the Suicide
of a Child

Mothers from the Albuquerque
Survivors of Suicide Support Group

A Mother's Heart:
Poetry and Prose to Comfort a Mother's Heart after the Suicide of a Child

by Mothers from the Albuquerque Survivors of Suicide Support Group

ISBN 978-1721834228

All proceeds from sales of *A Mother's Heart* are donated to SOS, Inc.

Editor, Desiree Woodland
Albuquerque, New Mexico
www.sosabq.org

Dedicated to SOS Mothers Everywhere

*May our words bring you comfort and solace
and provide a resting place for your heart.*

ALBUQUERQUE, NEW MEXICO

The loss of one's child is profound and devastating. Sadness is woven into our every smile, hidden in every joy, and acknowledged with every beauty. It travels with us like a well-worn coat. But we no longer despair; rather, we are filled with gratitude because we are not alone. There are others who have known the same sorrow and learned to live again. Opening our hearts, we learn the lessons of grief from one another. This hard-won wisdom nourishes our souls ... the alchemy of grief.

Contents

My Reed

by Rose Anaya

Her joys and sorrows were immense.

Talents were many, she hoped and loved with great intensity
and was my forever DIVA FASHIONISTA.

Loving the art of dance on ice or tapping on the studio floor,
the crayon on the canvas page, the summer fragrance
of carnations pink and the color yellow.

She reigned high when it was good and rode low when
it was sad.

Leaving many mourning with much to ponder about her
secret life.

This is known; not wanting to return to this everyday life.

Where she can NOW soar above in the everlasting.

Broken River

by Desiree Woodland

Shards of broken glass

Memories of a river

Lay upon a wall

A place to unburden my grief

Mother and father

Sister and friend

Working side by side

The groans of nature

Ground, where no living thing will grow

Crows startle and crack open the grey sky

Portend the coming of winter

We are all watching, waiting, hoping for some miracle

Small rooms where

Hordes of mourners cross neighborhood streets to gather

A procession for those left behind.

Sharp, cutting looks from the ones who don't understand

Suicide cuts a deep hole

As deep as a river

But not so deep that God's love couldn't find you.

A Quienes Partieron Sin Decirnos Adios

by Ana Friedlander

Dedicated to my son, David

El Universo Jiraba en su loco vaiven

Cuando desidio pararlo, con su temprana partida.

Se nublo el cielo y las cosas perdieron su color

En nuestras vidas todo perdio su valor.

Hoy a pesar del tiempo no logro despertarme

De este terrible sueño.

To Those Who Left Without Saying Goodbye

by Ana Friedlander

Dedicated to my son, David

The Universe revolved in its mad swaying

When he decided to stop it, with his early departure

The sky turned dark and all things lost their color, in our lives everything lost its value.

Today, despite the time, I cannot manage to wake up from this terrible dream.

Comfort for Today
Hope for Tomorrow

By Carolyn Bucklen

When I lost Adam, my life slammed into the wall, challenging my purpose, my very reason for being. I still struggle, almost frozen in this space, but live in hope that one day the shattered pieces will come back together with renewed vigor and new meaning. This struggle is represented by the difficulties I had creating this arrangement from the selection of the plant materials, plus 15–20 minutes of my limited design time spent in self-doubt; overwhelmed by the utter hopelessness of figuring out how to position the 2 multi-sided, awkward containers of somewhat irregular height into a stable, attractive configuration that I was attempting to combine for the first time—symbolizing my husband Roger's and my efforts and search for meaning in life as it is today. God speaks to me through nature. I interpret the message in this arrangement as comfort for today and as hope for tomorrow.

Kassy's Kause

by Susan Aguayo

On March 22, 2015 my daughter Kassandra A. Williams moved on from this world. The reason why I say moved on is although she is not here physically, she is here spiritually. Suicide was not a word we even thought about at home. Kassy was a college student who had just become a wife and decided to put college on hold so her husband could finish college. She was the only one working, and soon after her marriage found out she was expecting. This news was a surprise, but also a blessing because she always wanted to be a mom. Right before learning of her pregnancy, she lost her puppy to Parvo. It was devastating news that seemed to overwhelm her good news.

My daughter was not only beautiful on the outside but also on the inside. She loved life; she loved her family and most of all she loved where her life was headed. Although she seemed a happy and satisfied young woman on the outside, she was struggling with hidden depression on the inside. Her good news of becoming a mom became turmoil because her health changed during her pregnancy; she suffered from constant vomiting and bloody noses. She wasn't a sickly child and was always in control of changes. All this was new to her along with insomnia, anxiety attacks and mood swings. She felt confused why she couldn't feel happy and accept the changes of pregnancy. Instead, she felt irritable at everything and everyone. She lost weight and was dehydrated from all of the vomiting. I noticed how quickly she would get upset at situations, but thought it was normal to be hormonal under the circumstances. She questioned what was wrong with her because she had two older sisters with children and they hadn't felt this way. She also knew of my experience while pregnant, and nothing about our experiences seemed to fit hers. Her mood swings were taking a toll on her emotionally. I learned more of her struggles when her husband gave me her phone. I looked at her search history and saw all her questions and concerns. She tried to understand how it was possible to feel depression and anxiety while pregnant. Was it from a lack of sleep? Should she go to the hospital? Eventually she did seek help before taking her life, but they told her that what she was feeling was normal and sent her home. But, what she experienced is called perinatal depression. It is a serious condition and treatable, but only when recognized.

Now I question, "Are we educating enough to understand what can happen to women during pregnancy?" My research shows 20% of pregnant woman are documented as suffering from perinatal depression. I believe it's higher. That's how *Kassy's Kause* was born, a non-profit organization helping women find resources if they are experiencing this illness while pregnant. I also produced a documentary called *Kassy's Hope/ MyLife4Yours* with UNM and Lovelace Hospitals, as well as a panel of women sharing their experience with perinatal depression. Women need to know they are not alone.

Elegy of the Moon

by Desiree Woodland

Tonight as I look at the moon
My soul cries out for you
The stark contrast of white on endless black
Sharp as have and have not
Tonight, I can't find a way to remember you are with God
Only that you are not with me.

Hope

by Laura Burns

She walks across my vision
Right to left on the opposite sidewalk

Straight and slim, head thrown back
Chin leading a pale shock of hair—
One of the many shades of blonde she once assumed.

She walks in and out of the shop window that framed her
My breath catching, my heart stopping.

It isn't true that I will never see her again.
I will see her thousands of times in just this way—

Across a room, across a street.
I will freeze until she turns,
and I see it isn't her.

Until the hour when it is.

Enough

by Marion Waterston

I

They say that you're not really gone.
That you live on inside of me
My new silent partner.
Witness to empty days and restless dreams
But, I say—that's not enough;

II

I want you here—I want you now
I want my eyes to caress that face of yours,
my arms to hold your body
and feel the heartbeat that affirms life's presence.
I want to hear your sweet voice calling my name
Teasing me that way you used to do.

III

If only I had known
These simple moments wouldn't last.
Ahhh ... then I would have kissed them
And put them in a bottle and together

We would sail through the storms
Raging in my heart
If only I had known.

IV

Now I know—now I understand.
That life and love don't last forever
They are but fireflies in the night
And as their fleeting brilliance fades
They whisper, "Love now and love well."

V

So, my friend, you say, "That's not enough?"
Well, enough will have to be enough.
Learn that and move on.

Some Things Cannot Be Fixed

by Sandy Staplehurst

As I go through this journey, there are quotes and songs that speak to me. This quote was read at the Mom's support group.

> "Without a listener, the healing process is aborted. Human beings, like plants bend towards the sunlight, bend towards others in an innate healing tropism. There are times when being listened to is more critical than being fed."
>
> *Miriam Greenspan*, Healing Through the Dark Emotions

I think the reason this speaks to me is that I have realized that people's instinct is to fix the pain others are facing. Some things cannot be fixed, and what a person may need is just a good listener. To be listened to can be a great release of inner thoughts and feelings.

I talk to Josh. To some this may seem strange, but to me it's a continuation of conversations we had for the 38 years he was here. I pray he hears me every day when I tell him how much I love him ... and how much he is missed.

Our Journey

by Susan Pappas

My Precious Son

I felt our love as I carried you in my womb,
so deeply

I felt our love as I carried you in my arms, to take you
home after your birth,
so *deeply*

I felt our love as I rocked and sang to you,
so deeply

I felt our love as I carried you to the altar to be baptized,
so deeply

I felt our love as I watched you grow and experience life,
so deeply

I also felt your pain, as you struggled with your fears,
your anxiety, your confusion and later
your discouragement and depression,
so deeply

You were so fragile, yet so courageous
God blessed you with so many gifts: your music,

your voice, your big huge caring heart, your amazing mind, your wonderful laugh and sense of humor, your love and care for all living creatures, your compassion for and acceptance of the forgotten and marginalized fellow humans, and especially the gift of your love that you blessed our family with.

I felt so much of your love when you made recordings of your beautiful voice, for each of us and when you sang at your brother's wedding and my wedding,
so deeply

I felt our love and your pain, your agony, your confusion while holding you in my arms, as a man, while you sobbed because you believed you were a failure.
I hurt for you,
so deeply

I felt so much of our love when you shared your amazing accomplishments that touched so many lives,
so deeply

I felt so much of our love when you and I decided you would sing at my funeral, yet it was I who sang at yours.
It hurt,
so deeply

I could not carry you to the altar in my arms rather your sister carried you in your beautiful urn.
It shattered my heart,
so deeply

I am so grateful that you wrote us a letter and that you knew you were loved, that you expressed your love for all of us, so beautifully, yet so painfully. Yes, I am grateful for your letter, though it hurts,
so deeply

I am so grateful that I was blessed with the gift of your life for 44 years and today, I am truly grateful that you are no longer struggling, no longer hurting and suffering,

no longer needing to be so determined to overcome so many obstacles, so much injustice, no longer exhausted and worn down.

Today I still feel our love, the strong unbreakable bond that we will always have. Today I carry you everywhere I am and everywhere I go, not in my arms, rather in my heart full of love for you and in my mind, full of precious memories of you. I pray for you and I know you pray for me.
I miss you and always will,
so deeply.

My Prayer

by Sandy Staplehurst

When I first realized I was pregnant, you immediately became my world. You are still my world and always will be.

My prayer was that you be a healthy and happy baby. And you were.

As you got older my prayer was that you would be happy and know you are loved so very much.

As an adult my prayer was that you be happy in your career and confident in how wonderful you are.

Now that you are gone, my prayer is that I see you again. That is what I pray for.

You are my son whom I love more than anything else in this world. I miss your touch, your laugh, our relationship which I treasure, and your beautiful smile.

You are the first thing I think of in the morning, and the last thing I think of before I fall asleep.

You are my love!!

I Must Remember

by Marion Waterston

You are where you want to be
I must remember that.

You do not feel the healing warmth of sunshine
Nor April's cleansing rain.

No song of summer night birds
Can alter your tranquility.

The tumbling leaves of autumn
Lie forgotten on the hill.

Even winter's silver promises
Fail to woo you from your bed.

You do not miss these things, my love
I miss them for you.

And because they are for you
They are sweeter and more beautiful.

So, I will gather them like jewels and hold them close
And cover them with dreams.

Until that special day when I will find you
And we shall delight in them together.

Heaven's Gate

by Karla Tyrpak

God will take the tears I've cried
And create for you a river
You're sitting on that boulder now
A place to reflect, to ponder ....

It's peaceful there with no more strife
Free from all turmoil
Now you're truly alive ....

Though my heart is breaking
And my arms are empty
You're surrounded by green pastures
A place full of beauty.

So, my precious first-born son
I will wait for that day
To see and hold you once again.
Meet me at heaven's gate.

Not Just a Photograph

by Tammy Korman

He isn't just a photograph – an image on a wall
A story about yesterday – He isn't that at all
He wasn't all that different than anyone you know
His life was sometimes troubled – He seemed always
on the go
He had a life of chaos – He had his ups and downs
But he would soon recover when he'd see our
hurtful frowns
Our time together here on earth was truly meant to be
We had a special bond you know, my baby boy and me
The times we'd spend together – those special
childhood days
Some of my memories fading but will never fade away
I'll love that boy forever – forever and a day
He'd tell a joke and we would laugh a lot – he would sketch
a cartoon or two
He'd make such silly gestures 'cause that's what
he'd like to do
I wish you all had known him or even seen his face

I wish you could have seen his work or just
his dwelling place
He breathed the same air we all breathe – He loved
the same blue skies
The story of his childhood days brought teardrops
to our eyes
He sometimes said things that would make us think
what's truly on your mind
The answers to these questions are so very hard to find
What was it he was harboring? If only I had known the hurt
that he was suffering.
The pain that took him home
It doesn't make much sense to me why he would choose
to leave
I wonder what was on his mind, what was he to achieve?
Because we've all experienced a death so hard to take
The tragic way we've lost our love, no others can relate
The terrible way they took their lives how can we
ever heal?
Thank God for those who understand – you know the way
we feel
For some we go on suffering, while others shield their pain
That's okay with me – I won't complain – I just wish
I were the same
Will we ever understand – do we really need to know
the answers
That are hidden by the One who loves us so
I need not to explain how much I miss
my boy
For those of you – you've lost your love – your happiness –
your joy
To those of you who understand exactly how I feel
I pray for strength and hope or love – the only way to heal

They say that when we leave this world the answers will
be shared
Perhaps when that day comes to me my son will know
I cared
For if we doubt our hopes – our dreams – thinking death
is only death
There is no other way – we'll never ever find happiness –
We've already lost our way
We must speak up – we can't restrain from those struggling
to survive
Let's help to show the whole wide world it's good
to be alive!

In Loving Memory Tribute Pages

Maria Anaya

Maria Carmelita was born to me at 7:38 AM on March 11, 1988. She was the most beautiful baby girl I had ever seen, with her fair completion, shock black hair and big pools of chocolate eyes. I called her my Reedy, then as she grew, my Reed. I loved her then and I love her now so very much. She was the apple of her daddy's eye. Although shy as a young girl, she grew to be strong in her beliefs and opinions. Maria loved to draw fashion, to ice skate and dance. As a young woman she enjoyed the costume design of theatre where she met the love of her life, married & had a beautiful baby girl of her own. Maria was a wonderful mother. One love she had was cooking from old family recipes to create her own healthy and delicious dishes. She left this world on November 29, 2016 to join her loved ones gone before her, including her daddy, whom she always grieved. I miss her painfully and look forward with the hope of seeing her again.

Anne Alden Burns

Anne was just a little peach—a beautiful child and woman. She was lithe and athletic, creative and confident—she never doubted that her opinion was the correct one! I didn't know if she would be an artist, a lawyer, or a business woman—but I knew she would be successful.

She loved her camp in New Mexico, riding, and her Jeep. In college, Anne pursued her passions: history, design, and skiing. She traveled—seeing much of the United States, learning Spanish in Central America, and visiting her beloved Dali and other museums in Spain and Europe.

Anne started her career in fashion at Theory in New York and later at Barney's of New York. But she was thrilled to move to Washington, DC and become a buyer at the Smithsonian's Museum of the American Indian—the culmination of her lifelong interest in Native American arts.

We lost Anne to a disease called Idiopathic Intercranial Hypertension (IIH). After a valiant fight, there were no surgical or other options left to treat this painful and debilitating disease. Anne was not a person who would compromise with fate. Our precious girl, we miss you so.

Jonathan Tyler Burns

Jonathan was born on December 27, 1991 in Keflavik, Iceland. He had dual citizenship in the United States and Iceland, which offered him the option of attending college in Iceland at no cost had he ever decided to return to his place of birth. He will be remembered for his quiet, kind demeanor, his passion for baseball, his wit and contagious laugh, as well as his humility with the gifts God gave him. He was nicknamed 'cannon arm' by his baseball team in Bangkok, Thailand and was on the varsity team during his freshman and sophomore years. A fellow teammate wrote: "Never have I seen more humility in my life. You were modest about your talents." Additionally, this teammate mentioned that when Jonathan did anything noteworthy during a game, he would simply state, "It was nothing; I just did what I needed to do for the team." He carried a 3.5 GPA at the International School of Bangkok, where he attended school before he passed away. One of his teachers noted that "he was an astute, polite young man." He is deeply missed by all who loved him.

"I know well there is no comfort for this pain of parting: the wound always remains, but one learns to bear the pain and learns to thank God for what He gave—for the beautiful memories of the past and the yet more beautiful hope for the future."

— Max Muller

Jason Eisenberg

"In the end it's not the years in your life that count;
it's the life in your years."
Jason Eisenberg was a gifted artist whose passion
was sharing his creativity
with others. Today he lives on through the pictures
and illustrations he created.

David Friedlander

David Alexander Friedlander was born in Boston, Massachusetts on July 7, 1993. Although he spent most of his twenty years in New Mexico, he developed a fervor for Boston sports. David was a pleasant fun-loving child; he excelled at sports and loved the outdoors. He graduated from Rio Rancho High School where friends remember his big smile and caring nature. He enjoyed working with his Dad and brothers in the family business, and still found time to help Mom when her MS reared up. David's departure was far too early, and the grief still accompanies those whom he loved.

Greg Frost

Our relationship here on earth has changed forever, but you are still my precious son and I am still your mom. Our relationship will live in my heart forever, until we meet again.

Adam Matthew Paxton Hall

7/27/87 – 7/1/14

Josh and his mom

Joshua Scott Kliewer

Born: November 17, 1975
Left this world: January 29, 2014

Mark Waterston "Marko"
Born August 1970
Died June 1990

* Warmth and friendliness

* Laughter and sense of humor

* Compassion for those less fortunate

* Concern for the environment

* Basic goodness and decency

These were all parts of Mark. May his sweet memory
continue

to inspire us to acts of kindness, for the bonds of love
are everlasting.

Kassy Williams

Kassy was a beautiful, happy, giving young woman who thought of others' needs before her own. Her dream was to be a mom. She used to say, "I want to be a mom like you, Mom." I replied, "You will be a better mom then me." Her motto: "You can't buy memories, you make memories." She sure did leave me incredible memories.

Ryan Woodland

"I am Ryan Woodland. Born June 2, 1981. An artist, musician, mechanic, wanna' be engineer, car and stereo fanatic, thinker, skater, son, brother, and friend, whose pants were hanging just a little too low." Ryan was 24 years old when he took his life.

About the Survivors of Suicide Mothers

We are a group of mothers in Albuquerque who have found comfort and hope for living again after the loss of a child through suicide. In each other we have found life-long friendships and companions for the journey. We are mothers and wives, teachers, business owners, nurses, technical writers, therapists, and support group leaders. We are women who start movements to educate others and teach compassion for those left behind after suicide. But the job we cherish most
is that of *mother*.

www.sosabq.org

Made in the USA
Columbia, SC
29 July 2023

20826158R10029